THE SETBACK
FUELED
MY FAITH

Forgive the loss, surrender to the process,
cross over, and pursue purpose!

TANYA E. WILLIAMSON

The Scripture quotations are New Living Translation (NLT) from the Holy Bible, New Living Translation, copyright ©1996, 2004, 2007. Used by permission of Tyndale House Publishers, Inc., Carol Stream, Illinois 60188.

ISBN 978-0-578-60474-9
Library of Congress Cataloging-in-Publication Date is available.

Cover by P31 Publishing
Interior Design by Spirit Led Publishing & Printing Group
www.spiritledpublishinggroup.com

Legal Disclaimer
Although the publisher has made every effort to ensure that the information in this book was correct at press time, the publisher does not assume and hereby disclaim any liability to any party for any loss, damage, or disruption caused by errors or omissions, whether such errors or omissions result from negligence, accident, or any other cause.

Ordering Information
The Setback Fueled My Faith may be purchased in large quantities at a discount for educational, business, or sales promotional use.
For information email info@marriedtothering.com.

Request Tanya Williamson to Speak
Married to the Ring ® LLC
Mailing Address:
Post Office Box 1744, Wilmington, Delaware, 19899-1744
Email: info@marriedtothering.com
Office: 888.421.2220
Fax: 888.309.3306

TABLE OF CONTENTS

INTRODUCTION

I was quickly climbing the corporate ladder in the financial services industry. I had received countless promotions and earned a six-figure salary by the age of 30, which was a major milestone. Not to mention, being an African American woman labeled as a college dropout, having a child outside of wedlock, and being a byproduct of divorced parents – this was a huge accomplishment for me! There was absolutely nothing traditional about my entry into this market.

However, I knew that I still had some ways to go. I was not done! I knew in corporate America that being an Assistant Vice President was the highest achievement I could attain without a college degree. Meanwhile, I continued to attend several on-the-job leadership and training development programs to stay informed. **Career training, practice, and preparation were very important to me.** For this reason, I sought out mentors in leadership to shadow and familiarize myself with best practices from other industry leaders. I became an avid reader and read books by Stephen R. Covey, Jamie Dimon, John C. Maxwell, Marcus Buckingham, Dr. Donald O. Clifton, and many more thought leaders. In addition to those books, I kept what I believe was the most important book next to me: the Bible. Along with my Bible, I was building purposeful goals in the Purpose Driven Life book and workbook written by Rick Warren. At that time, I primarily focused on Scriptures for protection, safety, security, and prosperity. During this period, prosperity was becoming the most popular message being taught within the Christian church. Therefore, we were all fascinated by the Prayer of Jabez found in 1 Chronicles 4:9-10 which says, *"There was a man named Jabez who was more honorable than any of his brothers. His mother named him Jabez because his birth had been so painful. He was the one who prayed to the God of Israel, 'Oh, that you would bless me and expand my territory! Please be with me in all that I do and keep me from all trouble and pain!' And God granted him his request."*

Having a position in corporate America as an African American woman earning a six-figure salary was rare in the late 1990s and early 2000s. According to the U.S. Census, in the 1990s, only 8% of African Americans earned a six-figure salary (between $100K-$200K). In the early 2000s, there was a slight increase in this statistic from 8% to 12%. In 2014, the Center for American Progress cited that while women made up 54.2 percent of the labor force in the financial industry services, only 12.4 percent of those women were executive officers and 18.3 percent were board directors. As of today, there are no women CEOs in the financial industry. According to an American Banker article, as of 2019, the financial services industry is one of the last industries in which all the biggest companies are still run by men.

In saying this, I had beat the odds and labels of what others said was nearly impossible as a African American woman: securing an assistant vice president position during this period. I also changed the status quo for individuals who were raised in a single parent household. I personally counted this as a huge win for African American women, all women, single parents, my family, the Christian community, and, most importantly, for me.

Part I

THE SETBACK

Chapter 1

THE ANNOUNCEMENT

In 2002, I was at the height of my career. I was pulled into a meeting and told my department was closing and transferring to another location. I was offered the following packages:

- *Pkg 1:* Relocate to the local corporate office in an individual contributor role (not managing people) with the same salary and work on special projects;

- *Pkg 2:* Relocate to Maryland with a relocation package, bonus, salary increase, and child daycare expenses covered; continue to manage a segment of operations, with a strong possibility of being promoted to vice president; or

- *Pkg 3:* Accept the severance package.

I was surprised and completely caught off guard by the announcement. Throughout my tenure, I had traveled to other sites to assist with startups and site closures, so I had to ask myself why I did not see this site closure coming. I helped expand and restructure the department, and now we were closing it? This is all I knew. I knew that since I did not have an undergraduate degree, I did not have many options available with other competitors making the same salary. My choices were limited.

- For the very first time, the thought of previously dropping out of college before entering corporate America started to plague me. At that moment, I had a flashback to my father's face when I told him in the middle of my sophomore year at Delaware State College (now Delaware State University) that I was pregnant and coming home. I was entering into the workforce.

I started to recount in my head all the times I kept putting off my education, even when I felt that nudge to go back and complete my undergraduate degree. I kept telling myself that I was good. I had ignored the many opportunities presented to me to return to school because I kept receiving one promotion after another. For that reason, I felt like I had more time to return to school. <u>I had placed all my eggs in one basket</u> – this company.

Meanwhile, in the back of my mind, I anticipated that some of my direct reports and teammates would relocate with me. But when they visited Maryland, every one of them opted out of the relocation package. They asked me, "Tanya, are you sure you want to consider moving to this location? And if you do, are you going to be okay?" I responded with confidence,

"Sure will. The culture may be different, but I will be fine."

Call to Action:

Diversify your portfolio. Do not put all your talents in one basket.

<u>Here are some suggestions:</u>

- Pray about everything.

- Make sure you develop Smart Measurable Attainable Relevant Timebound (SMART) goals.

- Don't overlook your company's tuition reimbursement plan; leverage it.

- Explore multiple streams of income (residual income) and diversify your portfolio.

- Have a career progression & succession plan that includes other career or business possibilities.

Chapter 2

THE PRICE WAS RIGHT

The price ($) was right to relocate to Maryland. The salary, bonus, and relocation package were simply irresistible. I asked several questions. I was also able to negotiate some additional changes up front. My management team in Delaware was very accommodating. They immediately worked with the Human Resources department to make the necessary changes because they wanted to make this transition as comfortable as possible for my family and me.

The offer seemed perfect after I considered the cost. I was positioning my family into another socio-economic status, better schooling, and so much more.

Who could refuse that offer? I did not want to refuse, could not refuse, and had no intention of refusing the offer. In addition, the school district that my son would be attending ranked third in the United States, and he would be learning two languages. In the daycare my daughter would be attending, the children were reading, doing science, and working on math assignments. Where I came from, the children were being prepared for entry level positions; but these children were being prepared for entrepreneurship at an early age. It was very different than where I previously resided.

While carefully reviewing each option and thinking about my next role, I went home and started picturing myself in a vice president role. I set personal goals in my head with some very aggressive deliverables. I referred to past successes that I could mirror to map out how I planned to achieve the goals at the new location. I saw opportunity all around me. When opportunity knocks, go for it!

Call to Action:

Know your options and explore each one individually.

<u>Here are some suggestions:</u>

- Pray about everything.

- Know and ask clarifying questions about the relocation package (e.g. COLA).

- Create a contact/network list to stay connected with peers & leaders for future references.

- Identify your immediate personal and familial needs.

- Be open to negotiate so that you do not compromise your value system.

Part II

FORGIVE THE LOSS

Chapter 3

ON MY WAY UP

I signed the relocation acceptance letter. I was ready to relocate to Maryland, receive a pay increase, move into a new house, and emerge into the next role as a vice president. This was the perfect career move.

Right after I had made the decision, I had a dream. I awoke from the dream bothered and filled with anxiety because what I saw in the dream was quite alarming. It was totally the opposite of what I was believing for. I dreamt that I had lost my job, and asked myself had I made the wrong decision. I did not know what the dream meant, but I knew there was something significant about it.

I spoke with a Christian friend in ministry, whose specialty was dream interpretation, and I was told that my dream meant the total opposite. They told me that it meant that I would receive a promotion, not a job loss. I would be safe. This was exactly what I wanted to hear. Since I had sought out their expertise in the past, I trusted that the insight they provided would be accurate. For this reason, I was good. That meant I did not have anything to worry about. I proceeded with the move as planned.

Call to Action:

God used visions and dreams several times throughout the Bible to communicate with His people.

Here are some suggestions:

- Pray about everything.

- Don't limit the different ways that God can communicate with you.

- Know the difference between a dream and a vision.

- Journal or use a voice recorder to document the dream.

- Here are some examples of stories from the Bible of when God spoke through visions and dreams

Genesis 40 & 41; Genesis 15:1; Genesis 20:1-7; Genesis 28:10-17; Luke 1:5-23; Matthew 1:20, 2:13; Daniel 2:4; 1 Kings 3:5; Judges 7:12-15; 1 Samuel 3

Chapter 4

THE MOVE

After I arrived in Maryland and moved into corporate housing, I kept having several dreams. I have now come to understand that those dreams were step-by-step instructions that the Lord was giving me to assist and guide me through this particular season of my life. In the dreams, I saw signs of ease and dis-ease. I inquired about the dreams every now and then, and I stored them in the back of my mind.

One night I remember waking up out of my sleep soaking wet in fear. The type of fear or reverence that made me feel as if I could not let the Lord down. It was another dream. In this dream, I saw myself looking back. When I did, I lost everything. This time, I spoke with a few of my Christian friends about the dreams. They agreed and said, "Tanya, don' t look back!" I kept trying to figure out what was happening. I started telling myself, "Tanya stay focused. Do not look back!"

I returned to Delaware a few months later to attend a women's prophetic conference. At the conference, I experienced another encounter. At the registration table, each guest received a color-coded label on their name badge. Out of over 200 guests, the host asked everyone to go to their assigned group. However, my name badge did not correspond with any of the color-coded labels. When the host noticed this, she was shocked. She did not know how this had happened. The host turned to the guest speaker. Then, the guest speaker stepped down off the stage and asked if I could come to the front of the room. While standing in front of the room in front of over 200 guests, I felt extremely uncomfortable. She sensed that I was uncomfortable. I was uncomfortable because I am not big on people prophesying or speaking words of wisdom over my life in public settings. Plus, I had seen a lot of people damaged by false prophecy over a short period of time "I was very skeptical about this moment, yet I granted permission for her to proceed." She said the Lord showed her that although I was in casual wear and was not dressed like the other women in the room, I was a woman of wealth and plenty. She said, "You don't look like everyone else, and you try your best not to." She then said that the Lord was sending me to the mountains, and I was about to go through a season of separation. I would be separated from everything that was familiar to me. The Lord wanted me to deepen my relationship with Him and teach me His ways. He also wanted to heal me from past hurts. The Lord did not want me to carry or inherit ungodly practices, habits, beliefs, or behaviors learned from leaders in the church. The prophetess further said that this place where God was leading me would be extremely uncomfortable for me, but the Lord was developing and refining my character and removing those things that were contaminating me. She confirmed what I had already received insight on, but the words she spoke added clarity to some unanswered questions that I had before the Lord. She also said that I could only rely on the Lord in this next season of my life. She said no one would be able to help me, and that I would have to rely on Him to send each resource. She proceeded to say that although I was a woman of plenty, I was entering a season where everything around me was going to dry up. No one around me was going to be able to help me but the Lord. She also said that she did not see the man I was with on the journey with me. (She was referring to my first husband.) She wanted me to know that the Lord said He trusts me, and He was strengthening me completely from the inside out. I would eventually lose everything, but the Lord was going to restore everything back to me twofold. She closed by telling me not to become fearful along the way.

What this woman did not know was that she had sent confirmation. Although I had repeated dreams that I was losing, I had never had anyone tell me that I was going to lose everything.

I've learned that although I have been given insight to see some things, there is a timing for it all. We must know when to speak on certain topics. When she mentioned that the Lord was sending me away to the mountains, she was on point because I had moved to the mountains of western Maryland.

Call to Action:

Know the voice of the Lord for yourself.

<u>Here are some suggestions:</u>

- Pray about everything.

- Know the Word of God so that you can rightly divide the truth.

- Test the spoken word given to you to make sure that the prophecy aligns with God's Word.

- Join a women's fellowship group.

- Learn how to recognize an authentic word of affirmation.

Chapter 5

THE CULTURE

Months later, I was still having a difficult time adjusting to the new location's culture. I thought things would have settled for me by now, but that was not the case. I tried to find ways to proactively fit in and adapt, but it seemed as if all of my efforts were in vain .

The leadership style was aristocratic, and I had never worked in a remote location before, which did not help. The climate was very different than what I was used to. The transition started to become hard and lonely, especially since I had no family or friends to lean on. This was not at all what I had anticipated.

I previously met the manager who was temporarily assigned to me. We were introduced to each other virtually. Every now and then, she visited Delaware for leadership meetings. I knew very little about her because, often in the regional meetings that we attended, we were never assigned to the same team for follow up.

Her primary focus was to oversee the site's consolidation and transition plans. This was where most of her time was spent. As a result, scheduling one-on-one sessions was not on her radar, for which she often apologized.

She solicited help every now and then, if she thought I needed it. I completely understood the deliverables she had before her because I had previously worked on site consolidation plans, too. They could be overwhelming at times. Since she was not my permanent manager, she had very little involvement with the make-up of this site culture; she had transferred from another location down south. Because of my experience, she automatically assumed that I would hit the ground running and require very little management.

Being new to the site, the youngest, and the only African American woman assistant vice president (AVP), I needed some assistance. I was used to building a shared vision with my teammates, one where we all collectively agreed. I was used to expressing myself openly as we focused on establishing goals, values, and missions that were held across the department together.

Because of this style, it was obvious that the management team was minimally interested in the value that I was bringing from the headquarters. However, I felt that they viewed my position with them as a possible threat because no one knew whether this site would be next to close. The data at the time had shown that we were consolidating sites practically every two to three years. For that reason, some were more concerned about saving their position, instead of embracing synergy and collaboration.

When I offered ideas to automate certain processes to make things more efficient and convenient for the staff and our customers, each suggestion or recommendation was discounted. In other instances, I discovered that the ideas I had prepared were given to someone else to introduce to our executive leadership team. Everything I had tried to implement or follow through on with my direct reports was not considered or decided upon in a timely manner. This ultimately affected the timeliness of my responses to my direct reports, which was not good because I was a new leader at the site. Although I carried the title and position, it was obvious that my voice and opinion did not matter. It was as if, in so many words, management wanted me to know that I was not welcomed. It was in my best interest to quickly adapt to their way, or things would become a lot more difficult for me.

As a transformational, infectious, high-energy, and hands-on leader, I chose to redirect my energy solely on my team's performance. This allowed me to offset what was happening until I could find ways to adapt to the culture and its overarching leadership style. As my team began exceeding the key performance indicators, I was so excited. I could at least find one happy place. However, I was then pulled into the office and reprimanded for being so open-minded and informative with the staff.

Eventually my peers backed off from communicating with me to avoid any crossfire. They only had conversations with me if they had to respond in a meeting. Other than that, there was minimal dialogue. This was very different than working with my teammates and direct reports in Delaware. We embraced teamwork, collaboration, and synergy. We were used to putting out fires together and working long hours to get to solutions. Since they could sense what was going on from afar, they didn't dare to risk their status by getting involved. It felt like internal sabotage, but I just did not know how to handle it since everything around me was new. My leadership style was not welcomed, not to mention I was the only African American female AVP at this location. I was an emerging leader, and it appeared as if I was a threat to those who currently held vice president positions. It was obvious and brought about so many distractions.

Because of the pressure, I did what I said I wouldn't do. I started to slowly look back. I kept creeping back to what was familiar to me. I kept creeping back to my past wins and my peers who had remained in Delaware but moved into an individual contributor role not managing people. I did not like this place at all. I felt like I was all alone on this island – completely by myself. Loneliness crept in because I no longer felt as if I knew my purpose at the site. I started questioning everything around me, and the feeling of rejection brought about some unwanted insecurities. I never had an issue confronting conflict and providing constructive feedback and criticism until now. I did not know how to endure this type of conflict because I was not prepared. It was unexpected, and I did not have a support team in place. I did not feel comfortable discussing any of what I was going through with my past leadership because I wasn't certain what was being said behind closed doors from the new leadership. I was doing my best to minimize conflict, not burn any bridges, and save face!

The adage "People don't plan to fail, they fail to plan" certainly holds true, especially when it comes to major life events, such as a move. The relocation plan seemed perfect when it was offered. However, I began to realize that I had not done my due diligence on the workplace culture. The money diverted my attention from researching and investigating this matter.

Call to Action:

Are you struggling to adjust to a new work environment?

Here are some suggestions:

- Pray about everything.

- Make sure you know your leadership style, as well as those of your teammates and manager.

- Set up a 1:1 meeting to observe your manager's leadership style in real-time.

- Manage your goals and tailor them to align with your manager's key matrices.

- Make sure you are emerging from a personal vision to a shared vision.

Chapter 6

THE SET UP

Finally, I was told that one of my peers in Maryland had recently been promoted, so she was going to be my permanent manager. I had met her previously on past teleconference calls when I lived in Delaware. I knew up front that this was going to be a very interesting journey. Suddenly, a new opportunity presented itself to me! I was asked if I would work for the next six months on a conversion project. My name was given to serve as a subject matter expert on a special project which included some travel to Columbus, GA. Several experts from across multiple locations (regions) were being assigned to assist in this project, and I had been selected. Due to the pressure, I did not hesitate to jump on this project. My motto was "where there is adversity, there is opportunity to soar." In this case, I so badly wanted to return to Delaware – working on this project provided me with that.

I did not let anyone in Delaware know about the cultural challenges that I was experiencing in Maryland. I was too embarrassed and ashamed to say that I was having difficulties. I thought that sharing this would be catty and unprofessional. Therefore, I just kept my mouth shut and delivered what was asked of me throughout the entire project. I was so excited to be given an opportunity to work on this initiative. I knew that they knew my work ethic would speak for itself. Because of this, I mentally dismissed what was happening at the site.

On one occasion between my travels from Columbus, GA to Frederick, MD, I needed to head back to Delaware to provide a business update. While traveling to Delaware, one of my Christian friends in leadership contacted me saying, "Tanya, my car is down. Is there anything you could do to help me?" I didn't hesitate to help. I told him I would get back to him. After I investigated my options, I allowed my friend to use my car that I was storing in my garage in Maryland. Then, I secured a rental at the Philadelphia airport using my corporate credit card. I thought this was fine. I had to work in Delaware anyways, which was unrelated to me being at the Maryland office.

When I received the invoice from the corporate office, instead of submitting the request to the accounting department to pay, I paid for the rental on my corporate credit card with my personal credit card. I thought this would be okay; unfortunately, it was not. I knew that I was eligible for a rental, but I really did not need the rental because I had my car.

I thought I was doing something good, but this entire transaction backfired in my face. At the end of the project, when I returned from Columbus, GA, I was expecting to get recognized for all the work I had completed. Instead, I was given a pink slip informing me that I was terminated for using my corporate credit card for personal use because of this single transaction. No one asked me any questions, sought clarification, or offered any warning. Just like that – I was dismissed!

They waited until I completely transferred all the knowledge I had learned over the years into system specifications for future automation before they let me go. My position in operations was given to a Caucasian woman with tenure whose salary was half of mine.

It was evident that the entire story had not been told to the leadership team in Delaware, and no one wanted to hear my explanation. I was treated as if I had never existed in the company. Later that week, I received correspondence verifying the payment I had made, which confirmed I did not steal anything from the bank. However, it was a violation of the company's code of ethics. If given a chance, I would have been able to explain. But, I was not given the chance. My new manager was already looking for one technicality to get rid of my role in Maryland. Finally, she was able to use this against me.

Now I understood why she was never available for a one-on-one discussion. Although she coordinated the termination, she had the leadership team in Delaware facilitate it while I was working from that office. They could not speak to anything because they were only assigned to administer the termination.

They said the company's policy stated that using a corporate credit card for personal use was considered grounds for termination. Ultimately, I did not use it for personal use. It only appeared as if the corporate credit card was being used for personal reasons. In fact, I had plans to use my vehicle, but allowed my friend to use it instead. I chose to get a rental because I was traveling on business from Maryland to Delaware, which I could do under the company's travel policy. It appeared as if I was using my personal credit card because I chose not to submit the invoice to my manager for approval; instead, I made the payment using my personal credit card.

All of this could have been avoided, had I not allowed my feelings to interfere with my dissatisfaction and instead properly communicated in advance to management what I had done. In doing this, I opened the door to misunderstanding and miscommunication, which led to the ultimate betrayal. All of this was a misunderstanding. At this point, I realized that the enemy arrives in subtle ways. I later tried to argue the case with the Department of Labor, but it was right after the era with the big Enron case that happened in the latter part of 2001. There were new regulations and legislation being imposed across the entire financial industry, especially around corporate credit card usage. My manager developed her argument to present it as if it was a scandal. In fact, that was not the case. So much was running through my head.

I was sad and lost all hope. Therefore, I kept looking back and reflecting on my previous experiences. I faltered in perspective because I started making choices without consulting management. I was management, but I was being treated in a way that was indescribable. I started trying to figure out why I shut down.

As you can imagine, I immediately thought about that dream that I had following my acceptance of the relocation package. What God had revealed to me in that dream happened exactly how it appeared, and involving the same person who later became my manager. What I realized was that I did not need anyone to interpret the dream because the Lord was preparing and showing me exactly what was to come. He was forewarning me of the betrayal that would happen along the way.

I should not have allowed the pressure to distract me from purpose. Not only did the Lord share with me what was to come, He gave instructions along the way to not look back but to follow His steps. Instead, I looked back because of fear of the unknown. I did not trust Him wholeheartedly because of the level of discomfort I was experiencing in the process.

I recall a very familiar passage in 1 Kings Chapter 13 that closely related to my story.

There was a man of God who received specific instructions from the Lord. During his journey, he was confronted by a Prophet. The Prophet told him that he had a word from the angel of the Lord, that was contrary to the specific instructions that he had already received from the Lord. Because the Prophet told the man of God that the word came from the angel of the Lord, the man of God thought it was true. So, he instead followed the instructions of the Prophet. He later found out through the Prophet that it was a lie. The so-called Prophet came with intent to deceive him. The Prophet had his own ulterior motive. Because of the man of God's disobedience, God brought judgment and he lost his life.

Call to Action:

Find positive ways to communicate in difficult situations.

Here are some suggestions:

- Pray about everything.

- Be mindful of those who are trying to falsely build a perception of your performance.

- Provide weekly one-on-one updates to your manager on all projects.

- Obtain 360 feedback along the way from your peers, clients, and teammates.

- Be aware of your employee rights, and do not be afraid to notify HR.

Part III

THE DECISION

Chapter 7

CHANGED THE COURSE OF MY LIFE

Although I didn't physically lose my life, I lost my life. This one decision changed the entire course of my life. It suddenly changed my financial and socio-economic status. I went from a corporate executive to eventually becoming homeless. I kept asking myself how I had allowed this to happen. It was obvious that I did not follow each instruction that He provided to me. Instead, I listened to the heart of man and my own heart over the voice of God. Jeremiah 17:9 says, "The heart is deceitful above all things, and desperately wicked: who can know it?" The Lord told me not to look back, but I did because I tried to create my own way of escape. Therefore, I deceived myself out of overcoming and reaching another level in my life.

We must learn to accept accountability for the choices, contacts, and associations we have in our lives. The friend who asked me for transportation knew I was struggling emotionally in Maryland. He was very much aware of the attacks I was under, but in that moment he was looking for some relief from his test. I said I was rescuing him when, in fact, I needed to be rescued. I don't blame him because no one forced me to do what I did. But, in this learned a valuable lesson: seek God first when others are going through a test, too. It's okay to say no and not feel guilty about your response. You must be careful not to make desperate moves in your most vulnerable state. I thought maybe if I sowed into his life, because I am naturally a giver, some of the pressure automatically would be relieved. Instead, the pressure became greater! I was trying to use a principle of giving to bail me out of this moment and time in life.

In this lesson, I also learned that we cannot place people before God's instructions, regardless of their title in the church. There are no exceptions. When God has clearly given specific instructions, we must obey each step, even when others do not agree.

Call to Action:

Before you proceed, ask yourself, "what did God say?"

Here are some suggestions:

- Pray about everything.

- Learn the order of distribution and allocation of your expenses.

- Keep a pure heart with right motives in all that you do.

- Do not shift the blame; accept accountability for the part that you played.

- Do not compromise your values for anyone, regardless of one's position.

Chapter 8

Your Decisions Can Cost You

I paid a hefty price for this decision. I began to do the inner work and understand the real reason why I was working long hours. What was the underlying motive behind why I wanted to relocate to another state? What was I hiding from deep down on the inside? I seriously needed to get to the root of what had really happened.

I learned that although I was struggling to adapt to the new culture, having others around me that I relied on or who relied on me, did not make my transition easier. There is a level of emotional codependency between the two. I didn't realize that those back home were struggling with my absence, too. I was feeling the emotional connection of not only my feelings, but theirs as well. When there is an emotional bond, I have learned that it is very important to create a transition and expectation plan for yourself. When you do, there are some boundaries that you must establish so that you can clearly recognize when or if the dependency is getting in the way of you applying your faith.

When you go through changes in life, it's important to be informed about the stages that you will go through physically and emotionally. It's vital to replace the change with something equal to or of greater value; otherwise, there is a strong probability that you will revert to what you were used to.

You do not want to easily default to the old, especially when the Lord is calling you to something new. We must understand that it will be uncomfortable for each one of us, but we must obey. There is a stretching that comes with change. This is normal. For instance, think of yourself as a rubber band. Stretched rubber bands are loaded with so much potential. It takes a lot of expanding before the rubber band breaks. Each one of us is built with a lot of promise. Take a look at Genesis 1:28: "And God blessed them, and God said unto them, 'Be fruitful, and multiply, and replenish the earth, and subdue it: and have dominion over the fish of the sea, and over the fowl of the air, and over every living thing that moveth upon the earth.'"

When I moved to Maryland, this was the beginning of my separation from my first husband. I had every intention not to return and file for divorce. For so long, I had suppressed the fact that I did not want to be married. I got married for the wrong reasons. I was married because of a decision that I had made in the peak of my career when I was single and 26 years old. I had just flown back from Heathrow, Florida for work and was heading to a business conference in Washington, DC. I decided to take my first husband, who was just a friend of mine at the time, on the business trip with me. Surprisingly, a business trip turned into an unexpected pregnancy. An unexpected pregnancy turned into a marriage because I was too ashamed to bring a second child into this world without having a two-parent household. I knew better. I knew fornication was not acceptable. I already knew what it was like to have a child out of wedlock. Therefore, when he asked for my hand in marriage, I went ahead and gave it to him. He and I both knew I was not ready. Although my children are truly a blessing, I understood that there were still consequences associated with my sinful actions.

You see, sin causes an individual to make unwise decisions. You start to bypass very important stages of development within a relationship when you do things outside of God's order, which ultimately can cause undue harm to an individual's mental, physical, or emotional state. Since I was not mentally ready for marriage, I single handedly made choices as if I was still single (even though I was married). I withdrew myself on several occasions to avoid a decision that I had made, or I avoided having discussions with him because my transparency with him caused him to become even more irate. It was so toxic and stressful.

When the relocation opportunity came up two and a half years into my marriage, I saw it as a perfect opportunity to remove myself physically and mentally from having to address the decision that I had made. From day one, I was already tired of the blended family issues, the ex-wife's drama, and the fact that I was just not ready to be married. Although I was professionally savvy in business, I was not competent in marriage and had no interest in becoming competent. At the time, I was still very young and trying to find myself. I was not ready for that level of commitment. I found myself hiding behind my career instead of dealing with this area of my life. Altogether, I thought relocating was the best option for me.

Let's recap from the earlier chapter about how I felt when the prophet interpreted the dream and confirmed that it was okay to relocate. I felt a sense of release. I started thanking God for what I thought He was doing, which was providing me with a way of escape from a choice that I had made, not one that He had ordained. I took that scripture in I Corinthians 10:13 seriously: "The temptations in your life are no different from what others experience. And God is faithful. He will not allow the temptation to be more than you can stand. When you are tempted, he will show you a way out so that you can endure." For this reason, everything seemed to be coming together. All I saw in those verses was a way out!

So, I had to ask myself why I would return to an area that I was looking for an escape from. Why didn't I put closure to it the way God had instructed me to? Why did I keep the door open just in case things did not work out with the move? I knew things were not going to work out because I did it for the wrong reasons. I was not mentally ready for marriage, and I ended up marrying someone that I was not in love with.

What I did not know at the time was that when you have unresolved issues in your marriage, it leads to a downward spiral in everything else you do. At that time, I was ignorant to what the power of covenant meant. I did not know that it was the highest form of agreement on the earth. No one around me discussed what a healthy marriage looked like and learning more about it was not a priority on my list. The Bible says in Matthew 12:25 (MSG) "…a family that's in a constant squabble disintegrates." Honestly, I hardly knew any scriptures about marriage, had very little education involving how to build a healthy marriage, and my parents were divorced.

My heart's desires were only with my children and my career. The order of priority for me was God, my children, career, and then my husband. I had substituted my career in exchange for my covenant relationship with my husband. Although I did not engage in infidelity with another man, I had an affair with my career and hid behind my children because of the choices that I had made.

Looking back, from a biblical perspective, I was completely out of order. Being out of order was an open door all packaged in one. Let me explain why.

The bottom line is that when you make emotional decisions, you are easily influenced by idols. I did things like put my pastor's voice before my husband's. As a matter of fact, I had learned to ignore and dismiss everything my husband said to me. This is an example of idolatry.

To be perfectly honest, while on the journey to Maryland I remained honest with God, even when it all felt very uncomfortable. There were some areas I just was not spiritually mature in at the time, and I relied on others. I developed an emotional bond with my pastor, who was single, to provide me with insight, instead of searching the Word of God for myself. I also relied on the voices of others who were divorced, single, and overprotective of me because having a husband was a disservice for them. Since the relocation package felt so right, all I saw was "freedom." The move was my red ticket out of and away from a lot of things.

I heard the Lord say, "I am going to show you that it does not matter how much money you make, how much money is in your bank account, or how good your credit is. If I don't open the door, the door will not open." His word does not alter for anyone. He is a God of order and excellence. In Revelation 3:7 it says, "What He opens, no one can close; and what he closes, no one can open." James 3:16 says, "For wherever there is jealousy and selfish ambition, there you will find disorder and evil of every kind." I immediately looked up self-ambition. Self-ambition meant devotion to or caring only for oneself. It centered on being concerned primarily with one's own interests, benefits, and welfare, regardless of others.

This is when I learned that ignorance caused a series of unwarranted doors to open in my life; and that was never a part of His plan for my life. You become frustrated when you are not in alignment with His purpose. The very area He was blessing me in started to become a curse only because of my inability to address those things within that required immediate intervention. Dr. Scott Stanley calls this the spillover effect. The spillover effect happens when an individual's relationships become stressful and spill over into his or her personal life.

Call to Action:

Close doors properly.

Here are some suggestions:

- Pray about everything.

- When making decisions, question your motives.

- Put closure to all doors opened improperly, and remain honest with yourself and God.

- Learn how to build a shared vision selflessly.

- Ask yourself if you will be hurting yourself or others with your future.

Part IV

SURRENDER

Chapter 9

No Longer Relevant: From Comfort to Dis-Ease

First and foremost, the Lord never breaks a promise. You must realize when you initially enter new territory that you are not going to be relevant. You must establish a rapport. Although your potential has arrived, it still needs to be proven, refined, and groomed to adjust to the new environment.

Let's be very clear. When all your motives are right and, most importantly, you put the Lord first in everything, He will guide you with His instructions and hide you from the evil one. The Lord, quickly brought to my attention two familiar passages: Psalm 91:1 and Matthew 11:28-30. "Those who live in the shelter of the Most High will rest in the shadow of the Almighty."

He was telling me in so many words: "Tanya, come to Me because you are weary and burdened, and I want to give you rest. Take my yoke upon you and learn from Me, for I am gentle and humble in heart, and you will find rest for your soul. For My yoke is easy and My burden is light. Regardless of the dis-ease in this hour, be encouraged because, as you obey each step I give to you, always remember that you will be safe! Some things will hurt because I am allowing you to recognize what has grown in you. I have hidden you in the mountains to go through the pain. Endure the process, which will ultimately allow you to cross over successfully into My promises. But, the truth of the matter is that you must get rid of those characteristics that do not look like Me. It is your time to be healed and transformed completely from the inside out. It's all according to my plan and purpose so that you can fulfill your purpose. Although, it does not feel good, it will be good for you and your entire bloodline."

The Lord reminded me that He was separating me to fulfill my purpose. There were a lot of ministers being raised in the Gospel at this time, but for some apparent reason I always knew He was raising me for the marketplace. He was raising me to be a representation of what He looks like outside of the walls of the church.

Immediately, I slowed down so that I could pay attention to the details and align my soul, mind, body, and spirit into oneness. I continued to remain honest with Christ, despite how uncomfortable this position in Him was. I continued to cry out to Him the deepest areas of my concerns. In return, He revealed to me areas that required His immediate intervention.

In Psalm 61:1-2, David said, "Hear my cry, O God, attend unto my prayer. From the end of the earth will I cry unto thee, when my heart is overwhelmed: lead me to the rock that is higher than I." In those mountains, I continued to unleash what I considered to be the most hidden parts of my life to the Lord in prayer. Do you know that there is absolutely nothing hidden from the Lord? This self-reflection period was not for Him; it was for me. Self-reflection is one's ability to experience introspection and discover their intrinsic nature, motivation, and essence. Furthermore, introspection involves examining or observing your mental and emotional processes.

The more I learned about me, the more I learned about the open doors I had at that time. I confessed my sins, gave over my idols, and asked God to purify me from all unrighteousness. I laid aside my business acumen, minimized my comprehension, and removed myself from trying to analyze the One who created me. He already knew what was lying dormant inside of me, but He **wanted me** to recognize what was lying dormant so that the healing could begin. Although I was not an alcoholic, it was evident that the rules that they used in AA were very much applicable to me. I needed to replace those issues with key principles that would guide me along in this process.

I was so focused on getting my college degree to advance to the next level in corporate America, but deep down I was jacked up. You cannot keep piling up knowledge and not expect change to become relevant in your life. You will literally burst without application.

You must be okay with going into isolation, when appropriate. It is so important for you to discover the underlying truth about yourself and those behaviors and habits that are ungodly and may affect your future in the long term, if not properly addressed. I was reminded of Romans 8:1-8:

> *So now there is no condemnation for those who belong to Christ Jesus. And because you belong to him, the power of the life-giving Spirit has freed you from the*

power of sin that leads to death. The law of Moses was unable to save us because of the weakness of our sinful nature. So, God did what the law could not do. He sent his own Son in a body like the bodies we sinners have. And in that body God declared an end to sin's control over us by giving his Son as a sacrifice for our sins. He did this so that the just requirement of the law would be fully satisfied for us, who no longer follow our sinful nature but instead follow the Spirit.

Those who are dominated by the sinful nature think about sinful things, but those who are controlled by the Holy Spirit think about things that please the Spirit. So letting your sinful nature control your mind leads to death. But letting the Spirit control your mind leads to life and peace. For the sinful nature is always hostile to God. It never did obey God's laws, and it never will. That's why those who are still under the control of their sinful nature can never please God.

Always remember, the Lord is methodical in His approach. He is a God of order and excellence. Some things will not make sense to us, especially until we discover His truth. The relocation caused me to completely unleash and turn over every issue to the Lord in my journal or prayer.

In 1 John 1:9-10 it says, "But if we confess our sins to him, he is faithful and just to forgive us our sins and to cleanse us from all wickedness. If we claim we have not sinned, we are calling God a liar and showing that his word has no place in our hearts." As I remained in prayer, the Lord kept revealing to me those areas that **I chose** not to address. He let me know that I could no longer avoid any of them because the issues were either stemming from one another or piling up. To avoid something is the act of keeping away, or not doing it. This was my set time to change my position from avoidance to acceptance. Once you accept, you can ask for forgiveness, and then repent. Once you repent, James 4:10 says, "Humble yourselves before the

Lord, and he will lift you up. Do not compromise His standards to fit into others and the world standards."

When you are exposed to the truth (the Word of God), then light automatically shines into those dark places in your life. Light exposes the root of those things that are lying dormant in you. Although I was very conscious and aware of my bad habits, I would not work on eliminating them because I never knew when I needed to use them again. You are probably saying, "What do you mean until you needed to use them again?" Sin is sin. Some of us have pocketed certain areas. We have pocketed them if we have chosen to recover the act at some appointed time.

Simply put, there have been instances where I have tried to usurp the Lord in his decision-making by stepping into His lane. That is called control, and that is a sin. Stop fooling yourself, you too have the same issue. It says in Romans 7:18, "And I know that nothing good lives in me, that is, in my sinful nature. I want to do what is right, but I can't." Therefore, we must daily command our physical senses and body to fall into agreement with the Word of God.

In this circumstance, I had to understand the importance of getting rid of the bad and replacing it with the good. In Matthew 5:14-16 it says, "You are the light of the world – like a city on a hilltop that cannot be hidden. No one lights a lamp and then puts it under a basket. Instead, a lamp is placed on a stamp, were it gives light to everyone in the house. In the same way, let your good deeds shine out for all to see, so that everyone will praise your heavenly Father." People are watching you when you least expect it. They are conducting their due diligence and sizing you up. Therefore, you cannot allow a technicality to cause you to miss out on the plans that the Lord has spoken over your life.

Call to Action:

Put closure to matters.

Here are some suggestions:

- Pray about everything.

- Isolation is good when used for self-discovery and reflection purposes.

- Know the separation (grief) cycle and its order (denial, anger, bargaining, depression, acceptance).

- It's okay to seek professional counseling (e.g. Employee Assistance Program, etc.).

- Apply godly standards found in the Bible.

Part V

PURSUE PURPOSE

Chapter 10

Fueled By Faith: Now This Sense is Making More Cents!

I kept hearing "faith." Faith, faith, faith…. "Tanya, hold on to your faith throughout this entire process. Your belief in the Word will manifest at a deeper degree and your faith will be elevated to an entirely different level when you work My word, surrender, and rest solely in me. The more Word, the more faith."

The Lord revealed to me how to recover, rebuild, and secure prosperity, wealth, wholeness, and develop wholesome and healthy relationships by using faith principles found in His Word. I would like to reiterate something here. In the beginning of my journey as I moved up in corporate, the most popular message being taught within the Christian church was prosperity. Therefore, I was fascinated by how to build wealth only, without a solid foundation and some broken areas in my family framework.

Back then, I was asking God to enlarge my territory because that is what I was exposed to. And because He was fulfilling His word and territories were enlarging all around me by faith, I thought it was all good. I realized that the Lord did not want a family framework that was not solid. I'd like to call that a provisional blessing instead of a divine blessing. This time, that was not going to happen. I understood that I had to experience a demotion to clean up and refuel properly in order to truly reflect His attributes in every area on the earth.

In Deuteronomy 8:18 it says, "Remember the Lord your God. He is the one who gives you power to be successful, in order to fulfill the covenant [the promise], he confirmed to your ancestors with an oath." How do you get His power? In Joshua 1:8 it says, "Study this Book of Instruction [the Word of God] continually. Meditate on it day and night so you will be sure to obey everything written in it. Only then will you prosper and succeed in all you do." I learned in all of this that the key to gaining and sustaining the Lord's power was to obey everything written in the Word of God. I had to apply faith, which is our sixth sense that only functions in the spiritual realm, align my belief system (strategy) to activate my God-given authority (His power of the Holy Spirit dwelling in me) to cause those things that I was believing for to manifest suddenly on earth (properly)! This time, because of healthy resources (that He assigned), under healthy leadership (that He positioned), and through healthy associations (that He sent occupying with integrity), I could attract and sustain long term wealth to take care of your household and be a distributor to the Kingdom for His will to be accomplished successfully. It's not temporal. It reciprocates because it was established on good ground.

Honestly, I thought I had faith before this test. I learned that beating the odds and stigmas to climb the corporate ladder was the true success. Yes, that was one form of success, but God wants us to experience victory in every area of our lives, not just one! In my case, attracting and building the right relationships was key. Signs and miracles follow this level of impact.

Faith caused me to re-evaluate strategies quickly and develop coping mechanisms in advance. It also taught me how to proactively deal with rejection. I already knew that by faith the supernatural was about to happen against the common thought process of man. Because of my belief system, I was now prepared to walk in the room as the minority, instead of the majority. Why? Because the majority in the room still lived by the world's system, instead of God's system. The world's system is when one employs their natural five senses to guide them along the way, whereas the God system is when one employs the supernatural.

Often, I found people using their physical senses to guide and lead them in most of their affairs. We see this a lot on social media. Society has defined an influencer by the number of followers one has. However, the supernatural is where one believes in what they can't see, and they use God's Word and the Holy Spirit to see that very thing that they can't see to manifest from the spiritual into the natural. In doing this, one is programmed to only do, hear, and believe what God says, without compromise.

I had taken the necessary steps to identify, remove, and accept accountability for the choices that I made when I was operating solely out of the flesh (five senses). I started to grab hold of my belief system beyond the physical into the spiritual. Faith caused me to reprogram my mentality. This is when I received greater clarity to become thankful for being set aside, preserved, and forced into a position to confront and remove hindrances. I was trained by the Holy Spirit to recover, rebuild, and obey each step-by-step instruction.

I understand that in Genesis, Goshen was set aside for what was to come in the Bible. Even though Goshen was a place near the Promised Land, it was still Egypt and was not the place God wanted His people to establish a nation. He allowed the children of Israel to experience the misery of slavery to motivate them to move when the time came. Then, Moses was raised up!

God sometimes must allow us to experience defeat or pain in our Goshen in order to motivate us to leave the place that we are in because the promised land awaits. Wise people are willing to leave their spiritual Goshen and follow the Lord to His better place. But, in order to do that, you must operate out of faith. Once I understood misery was sent to motivate me to achieve the instructions the Lord had given me, I completely changed my posture and position.

I heard the Holy Spirit say, "Tanya, I want to show you how to receive success my way, which consists of a lifetime of neverending favor. Favor, which is far greater than an individual's financial, professional, socio-economic position, title, or status. I want you to draw nigh to me, listen to my instructions daily, and follow each instruction step-by-step, even when it is against every odd. I need you to go beyond what you've learned generationally, academically, and professionally to become like putty in my hands, having total reliance on me as your Father. I want you to believe that I will not fail you! I want to reveal to others through you as you believe in me by faith that there are no limits when you obey me with your whole heart."

At this point, my physical body felt as if it was going through a transformation. One that was, and still is, very difficult for me to explain to man. The Lord was unraveling my learned behavior from the emotional sense to pure God sense. I knew He created us with five physical senses: sight, hearing, touch, taste, and smell. But, I could not explain the scent of this sense. It was indescribable, but so refreshing.

The sixth sense is faith. This sense is required in order to operate in the spiritual realm with the Holy Spirit. In Hebrews 11:6 it says, "And it is impossible to please God without faith. Anyone who wants to come to him must believe that God exists and that he rewards those who sincerely seek him."

I had to unlearn everything that was ungodly and reposition it solely on God's Word. But I did not know what was ungodly until I got in the Word of God for myself. I had no enablers in this season; everyone had been removed. The Lord showed me through His

Word how to rewrite the narrative to coincide with His plan. His desire for me was to present all my plans first to Him, trust Him, and wait for His instructions and assigned resources. Through this, my belief system has elevated to a similar degree as that of what He promised Moses in Joshua 1:3: "Wherever you set foot, you will be on land I have given you."

Now, by faith, go back, reclaim your territory, and leave a legacy for your children and their children…. Amen.

Call to Action:

Go recover all!

Here are some suggestions:

- Pray about everything.

- Follow your customized roadmap.

- Never give up!

www.ingramcontent.com/pod-product-compliance
Lightning Source LLC
Chambersburg PA
CBHW031224090426
42740CB00007B/691